Fort McHenry

NATIONAL MONUMENT AND HISTORIC SHRINE

BALTIMORE, MARYLAND

Produced exclusively for Evelyn Hill
Evelyn Hill Corporation
Fort McHenry Gift Store
2400 East Fort Avenue
Baltimore, MD 21230

Designed in USA • Printed in China • 10G0077

© 2012 Designed and Published by Terrell Creative
6100 E. Connecticut Avenue
Kansas City, MO 64120

ISBN-13: 978-1-56944-433-7

Cover: Select photos Courtesy National Park Service, © Kent Larson and by Joe Luman © Terrell
Creative; Title Page and Back Cover: Photos Courtesy National Park Service; Inside Back Cover:
Photo © Kent Larson; Page 4, 11, 43 and 45: Photo by Kelly Elliott © Terrell Creative; Page 6: Image
courtesy Independence National Historical Park; Page 10: Baltimore American & Commercial Daily
Advertisers, November 16, 1813; Page 14: Courtesy of and © The Company of Military Historians;
Page 16: Lt. Col. George Armistead portrait Courtesy of the Maryland Historical Society; Pages 19
and 27: Maps Courtesy National Park Service; Page 28, 31 and 40: Courtesy Library of Congress;
Page 35: Star-Spangeled Banner Flag Courtesy Smithsonian Institution; Page 38: Photo by
Joe Luman © Terrell Creative

It had been almost a year since the "shot heard around the world" had been fired at Concord, Massachusetts in 1775. In the spring of 1776, while the Continental Congress debated the issue of independence, Marylanders in "Baltimore Town," (Baltimore was incorporated as a city in 1797). witnessed the approach of a British sloop of war as she sailed up the Patapsco River. She soon departed, but her presence raised serious questions about "Baltimore's" defense.

An earthen "star fort" had been erected by citizens on the tip of Whetstone Point, three miles below the town. Whetstone Point had long been regarded as a strategic military site to protect the water approaches to "Baltimore." A few cannons were mounted and troops under Captain Nathaniel Smith occupied the Fort, but no shots were ever fired during the American Revolution.

By 1781, when the combined French-American army passed nearby on their way to Yorktown, Virginia, the Fort, consisting of a water battery, (a group of cannons aimed over the river), powder magazine (a structure for storing gun powder) and barracks, had all but been abandoned. With the successful conclusion of the war in 1783 and the resumption of peace, the earthen Fort Whetstone was left to decay.

Britain's loss at the Battle of Yorktown in 1781 marked the beginning of a new nation in the United States of America. However, not even three decades later after signing

Courtesy Library of Congress

the Treaty of Paris, the two countries were at odds again.

Concerned for the city's safety, in 1793 the Maryland Legislature authorized the governor of the state to grant permission to the federal government "to erect a fort, arsenal or other military works" on Whetstone Point for the public defense. The following year, Congress likewise, authorized the initial construction of 16 forts, under the newly established War Department, to protect our maritime frontier from European aggression.

In 1798, unstable relations with France, which was in the midst of its own revolution, entered the United States into a Quasi-War (1798-1800). Although the war was limited to naval actions, Congress subsequently passed legislation to upgrade the country's land-based defenses. These defenses would be tested in 1812 with a second war with England.

ABOVE: Map of Whetstone Point showing "star fort" and shoreline batteries, 1792.
OPPOSITE PAGE: The entrance to Ft. McHenry, the Sallyport, is the only way in and out of the fort.

Part 1

THE EARLY YEARS, 1798-1811

Fort McHenry is probably one of the best-known American forts in the United States today. This is due primarily to its association with "The Star-Spangled Banner" during the War of 1812. James McHenry, for whom the Fort was named, was an Irish-born soldier and statesman who co-signed Maryland's ratification of the federal constitution, and

served as Secretary of War from 1796 to 1800 under the presidential administrations of George Washington and John Adams.

At the time of the Quasi-War with France, work began in Baltimore on a star-shaped fort with five bastions. French engineer Jean Foncin oversaw construction of this brick-faced fort, which enclosed a powder magazine and

BELOW: Map showing Fort McHenry in 1814
OPPOSITE PAGE: James McHenry, for whom Fort McHenry was named shortly before the 19th century. James Sharples, Sr., pastel, c. 1795.

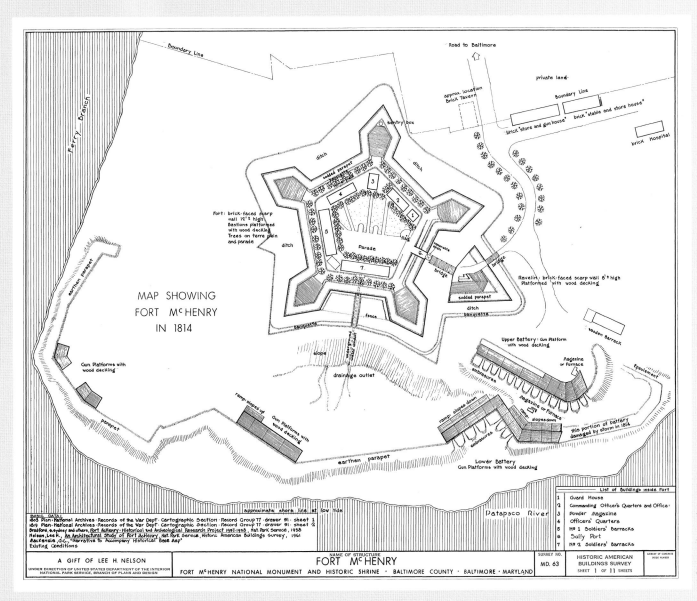

MAP SHOWING
FORT McHENRY
IN 1814

	List of Buildings inside Fort
1	Guard House
2	Commanding Officer's Quarters and Office
3	Powder Magazine
4	Officers' Quarters
5	N° 1 Soldiers' Barracks
6	Sally Port
7	N° 2 Soldiers' Barracks

A GIFT OF LEE H. NELSON
UNDER DIRECTION OF UNITED STATES DEPARTMENT OF THE INTERIOR
NATIONAL PARK SERVICE, BRANCH OF PLANS AND DESIGN

NAME OF STRUCTURE
FORT McHENRY
FORT McHENRY NATIONAL MONUMENT AND HISTORIC SHRINE · BALTIMORE COUNTY · BALTIMORE · MARYLAND

SURVEY NO.
MD. 63

HISTORIC AMERICAN BUILDINGS SURVEY
SHEET 1 OF 11 SHEETS

barracks. McHenry had employed Foncin to improve upon two earlier designs put forth by French engineer-artillerists Major John Jacob Ulrich Rivardi and Major Louis DeTousard, whose own designs were left incomplete due to a lack of funds. By 1802, the Fort was completed, and was garrisoned by troops under Captain Staats Morris. In the following years, work continued on several service buildings outside the Fort.

Of particular interest during this period was the organization at Fort McHenry of the U.S. Army's first mobile, horse-drawn artillery company (U.S. Regiment of Light Artillery) in 1808. Commanded by Captain George Peter, the company proceeded to the nation's capital "at the rate of five or six miles per hour" to demonstrate their maneuverability to war department officials.

This display of military activity and congressional legislation for raising additional troops was heightened by the Chesapeake-Leopard incident in 1807, which involved the British Frigate *Leopard* seizing three American sailors after issuing a naval broadside (firing cannons from one side of a ship) at the unprepared U.S. Frigate *Chesapeake*. England's

unchallenged naval superiority at sea, her presence in American territorial waters, the boarding of American merchant vessels and the subsequent impressment of our sailors embittered many Americans.

From 1809 until the declaration of war with England in 1812, President James Madison's administration attempted to secure diplomatic recognition of American maritime rights and citizenship. In Congress, the British were accused of inciting Indian warfare in the West. Newly-elected congressmen known as "War Hawks" (primarily from western states)

advocated war against Great Britain and the annexation of Canada. Congressmen, primarily from New England, bitterly opposed going to war at this time. They believed that attacking the British colonies of Canada was unjustified and that the U.S. military lacked the capacity to fight such a conflict.

On June 18, 1812, the War Hawks won the vote by a slim margin and Congress declared war on Great Britain. The young United States was militarily unprepared and divided internally. She was now to face the most powerful nation in the world.

Fort McHenry

To Reputable Young Men, will be given a *bounty of FORTY DOLLARS*, and 160 Acres of LAND, for enlisting in the 3d Regiment of Artillery, by applying to GEORGE ARMESTEAD, Fort McHenry.   Major 3d Artillery. aug 23   d

Soldiers at Fort McHenry during the War of 1812 shared many similarities with their counterparts in other theaters of the conflict. Generally, most were young, between 19 and 25 years old. Service in the regular army was voluntary. Some joined out of patriotism, others for the generous land bounties (160 acres) given upon discharge. At eight dollars per month, pay was considered low even by the standards of the day, however, recruitment bonuses of $150 prompted some to enlist.

A soldier's basic outfit comprised of a blue woolen single-breasted short-tailed coat, known as a "coatee," two pairs of linen pants and shirts, a black leather hat known as a "cap," two pairs of leather shoes and a tight-fitting leather collar worn around the neck called a neck stock and nicknamed "the choker." Additional items, known as accoutrements included leather belts which carried the three-pound bayonet, an ammunition pouch called a cartridge box and a knapsack, containing a blanket, extra clothing and personal items. A bag to contain food known as a haversack, and a canteen would be issued for a long march. In style, American soldiers closely resembled their British and French counterparts.

Photo by Kelly Elliott © Terrell Creative

ABOVE: A recruitment notice for the Baltimore papers from Major George Armistead, U.S. 3rd Regiment of Artillery at Fort McHenry

RIGHT AND OPPOSITE RIGHT: The recreated soldiers' quarters, which also include uniforms and weapons, realistically portray their living conditions.

Compared to fighting along the Canadian border, soldiers at Fort McHenry led an easier existence. They were housed in brick barracks, slept on straw mattresses and only faced combat once, during the bombardment in September, 1814. Located near Baltimore, they had access to all the entertainment that a large city could provide although, like most soldiers of the war, had precious little free time to take advantage of it. Rations included salted meats, primarily pork, as well as rice, peas, bread and occasionally cabbage when in season. One gill (quarter pint) of whiskey was given each day as a treat.

LEFT: Sixteen soldiers would occupy a barrack and they would sleep four to a bunk.

BELOW: This exhibit illustrates an independent artillery company, The Baltimore Fencibles. They represented the elite of the city's mercantile society who were well trained in the use of artillery and had much to lose should the British capture the city.

MANNING THE GUNS

BELOW: Powder barrels and boxes were stored in a powder magazine that protected gunpowder and ammunition from moisture, sparks and impact.

Proficiency and care for the fort's artillery was the primary responsibility for the regular soldiers. The 110 men of Captain Frederick Evan's Company of the U.S. Corps of Artillery spent the summer of 1814 practicing artillery drill and making ammunition for the cannons and muskets. Artillery at this time was classified by the weight of solid iron balls they fired. For example, a small field cannon known as a "Six-Pounder" would fire a round ball of that weight. In 1814, Fort McHenry possessed over 65 cannons, the largest fired cannon balls or "shot" weighing 18, 24 and 36 pounds. Although primitive by modern standards, the fort's largest guns could fire a 36-pound shot almost a mile and a half at a velocity of 1,600 feet per second. The solid shot did its damage by force of impact. During the summer of 1814 the fort received many reinforcements and during the battle, approximately 1,200 soldiers—professional and militia—manned the fort's defenses.

Photo by Brad Hill

LEFT: The maximum range of Fort McHenry's cannons was 1.5 miles. The British cannons had a range of 2 miles and their rockets had a range of 1.75 miles, but neither were accurate. Despite the approximately 1,500 British bombs and Congreve rockets fired at the fort, U.S. soldiers were able to defend their fort with little damage.

BELOW: During the major improvements made to the Jr. Officers' Quarters and Powder Magazine, in the 1830s, a second story was added to the barracks. Also, two new guardhouses on each side of the sally port were added to replace the old ones.

Part 2
THE WAR OF 1812

The War of 1812 got off to a bad start. The American offensive into Canada was met with defeat and humiliation due to poor leadership, ill-conceived campaign strategies and the inability of raw recruits to fight in an organized manner. Fortunes changed somewhat in 1813 as American offensives in Canada led to the burning of York (present-day Toronto) and a key naval victory on Lake Erie. Ultimately however, the British turned back American offensives into Canada, burned Buffalo, New York and secured the Saint Lawrence River. To take the pressure off of Canada, the British used their superior naval forces to threaten U.S. cities along the eastern seacoast. War came home to many Americans in 1813 when a large British naval force sailed into the Chesapeake Bay.

BELOW: The British naval force aiding Canada in the Chesapeake Bay, *H.M.S. Shannon Leading Her Prize the American Frigate Chesapeake into Halifax Harbour,* by John Christian Schetky, Ca. 1830, hand-colored lithograph

OPPOSITE PAGE: *The American Soldier, 1812* The Regiment of Light Artillery, an elite horse artillery corps, ranked first among the combat units in the Army.

WAR COMES TO MARYLAND, 1813

"The American navy must be annihilated: her arsenals and dock yards must be consumed: and the turbulent inhabitants of Baltimore must be tamed with the weapons, which shook the wooden turrets of Copenhagen." This editorial in the London Evening Star in the spring of 1813 was appropriately directed toward Baltimore, the third largest city in America, because of its burgeoning shipping industry.

In the first six months of the war, citizen-entrepreneurs outfitted armed private vessels, known as privateers, to distress and harass England's merchant fleet. Damages from this venture cost England's merchant class millions of dollars. In March of 1813, Rear Admiral George Cockburn arrived to enforce England's naval proclamation. In the ensuing months, British warships cruised the Chesapeake Bay attacking towns and communities whose citizens retained munitions of war, while establishing a naval base to survey the defenses of Baltimore, Annapolis and Norfolk, Virginia. Samuel Smith, U.S. Senator and Major General in the state militia, directed the defenses of Baltimore. With the assistance of Major George Armistead, the Fort McHenry's commander, preparations swung

into high gear. By the summer of 1814, entrenchments were dug around the city, cannons were mounted at Fort McHenry and additional forts and redoubts (small, usually temporary forts that support the main one) were completed around the harbor to support Fort McHenry and to guard Baltimore's marine entrance.

MAJOR GEORGE ARMISTEAD 1813-1818

Born in Caroline County, Virginia on April 10, 1780, George Armistead entered the U.S. Army in 1799 with a 1st Lieutenant commission signed by Secretary of War James McHenry. From 1801 to 1806 he served along the Canadian frontier at Fort Niagara, New York. He was made a captain in 1809 and was ordered to Fort McHenry, where he remained until he was reassigned to Fort Niagara in 1812. He soon received a promotion to major of the 3rd Regiment of Artillery and subsequently distinguished himself at the capture of Fort George, Upper Canada.

THE CHESAPEAKE CAMPAIGN, 1814

On April 6, 1814 in Paris, France, Napoleon Bonaparte was overthrown and was sent into exile on the Isle of Elba off the Italian coast. This peaceful pacification of Europe offered England a means to end the war in America with approximately 14,000 veteran soldiers of the Napoleonic campaigns. An estimated 4,500 of them were sent for a diversionary raid in the Chesapeake, the others to the main offensive on Lake Champlain.

To support the offensive, Vice-Admiral Alexander Cochrane, the Commander-in-Chief of British naval forces in America, issued an extended embargo to New England from his

naval base in Bermuda on April 25th. With the entire coastline of America now blockaded, it proved an effective economic measure and brought the United States to the edge of financial bankruptcy.

On June 1, 1814, a British expeditionary force commanded by Major General Robert Ross departed the French coast for a rendezvous in Bermuda, where Admiral Cochrane awaited with additional troops and ships. Together they sailed for the Chesapeake, arriving on August 16th. Combining their forces with Rear Admiral George Cockburn, who awaited their arrival, some 50 British warships and 4,500 troops were made ready for a possible strike on Washington in retaliation for the American burning of York, Canada a year before.

On August 19th, the British army landed at Benedict, Maryland where a road led to the nation's capital fifty miles away. In route, a British flotilla advanced up the Patuxent River, and in cooperation with the army, they forced the destruction of Commodore Joshua Barney's U.S. Chesapeake Flotilla on August 22nd.

On August 24th, they encountered the hastily assembled American army, mostly militia, defending the capital at Bladensburg, Maryland. They easily defeated the American army, and that evening the British, led by Admiral Cockburn and General Ross, torched the White House, the Capitol, and other federal buildings. The only heroic stand was made by Commodore Barney's command of 500 flotilla-men and U.S. Marines, who repulsed three British advances but were soon forced to retreat without adequate support. An observer wrote: "the militia ran like sheep, chased by dogs."

That night in Baltimore, citizens gathered on Federal Hill and soldiers stood on the walls of Fort McHenry, watching as the fiery glow of Washington lighted the skies. The next day, as remnants of Maryland's militia troops returned to Baltimore, the British returned to Benedict, boarded their transports, and sailed into the Chesapeake. Their next objective was Baltimore, which the Royal navy regarded as "the prize of the Chesapeake."

PREVIOUS PAGE: *Lt. Col. George Armistead,* Oil on canvas by Rembrandt Peale, 1817.
LEFT: *Capturing and burning of Washington by the British,* in 1814

17

⭐ BENEDICT

At this small Patuxent River town on August 19-20, 1814, 4,370 British troops landed. British pickets occupied the crest of the ridge to the west while the troops were encamped below it on the north side of the road. This invading army defeated the Americans at the Battle of Bladensburg and burned Washington D.C., returning to Benedict to re-embark their ships on August 29-30, 1814.

⭐2 LOWER MARLBORO

During June, and again in August 1814, the British took "quiet possession" of this tobacco port town along the Patuxent River. Local folklore claims that a young boy convinced the British that a hornet's nest was a rare hummingbird nest. The British took the nest aboard ship and when the nest was opened, the hornets attacked and local residents witnessed Admiral Cockburn and a dozen of his officers dive overboard.

⭐3 MOUNT CALVERT

Finding the U.S. Chesapeake Flotilla had been scuttled just up river, Rear Admiral George Cockburn Commander of the British naval forces on the Chesapeake, dis-embarked his seamen here to join the expeditionary forces marching on Washington D.C. There is a spectacular view of the Patuxent River from this 1790 Federal-period house.

A Chesapeake Bay Gateways Network Site
www.pgparks.com/places/parks/mtcalvert.html

⭐4 UPPER MARLBORO—Beanes' Grave/House Site

It was in this town that the British Army and Navy met on land for the first time during the campaign. At the home of Dr. William Beanes, good friend of Francis Scott Key, British Rear Admiral George Cockburn convinced Major General Robert Ross to attack Washington. Beside Beanes' house, which burned in 1855, is his grave.

⭐5 BLADENSBURG WATERFRONT PARK

This park provides a good view of the bridge site where the British forces crossed the Anacostia River and attacked the first line of the American defenses during the Battle of Bladensburg on August 24, 1814.

A Chesapeake Bay Gateways Network Site
www.pgparks.com/places/nature/bladensburg.html

⭐6 WASHINGTON D.C.

After defeating the Americans at the Battle of Bladensburg, the British captured Washington D.C. and burned many of the public buildings including the Capitol and White House on August 24, 1814. The British burned the buildings in retaliation for the American burning of York, the provincial capital of Canada, on April 27, 1813.

⭐7 ALEXANDRIA

After surrendering itself, the city was occupied by British naval forces from August 28 through September 3, 1814. From Shooter's Hill, where the George Washington Masonic Temple now stands, President James Madison met with others to plan counter measures for attacking the British fleet as it descended the Potomac River.

Photo Courtesy Library of Congress

RIGHT: Detail, *Sir George Cockburn, Admiral of the Fleet, pictured by the flames of Washington.* Painting by John James Halls, 1817

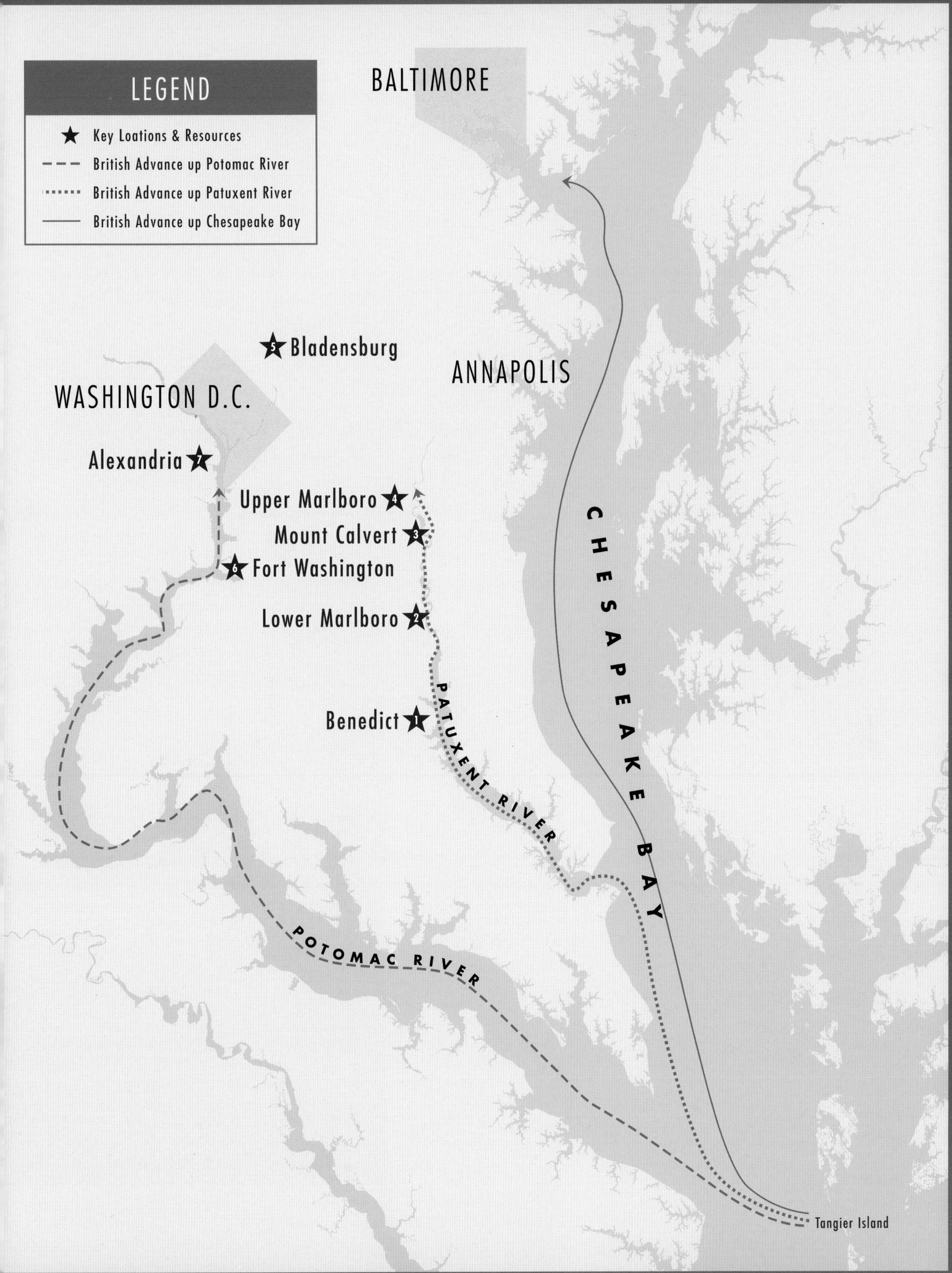

BALTIMORE

LEGEND

★ Key Loations & Resources
--- British Advance up Potomac River
⋯ British Advance up Patuxent River
— British Advance up Chesapeake Bay

ANNAPOLIS

★ Bladensburg

WASHINGTON D.C.

Alexandria ★

Upper Marlboro ★
Mount Calvert ★3
★ Fort Washington

Lower Marlboro ★2

Benedict ★

PATUXENT RIVER

CHESAPEAKE BAY

POTOMAC RIVER

Tangier Island

THE BATTLE OF BALTIMORE 1814

In the early 1800s, Baltimore was a prosperous inland seaport with 50,000 citizens. By the time of the War of 1812, Baltimore had reached its peak in the shipbuilding industry and was prospering as a newly incorporated city. This, combined with its central geographic location to western farmlands, water mills, and a deep freshwater harbor, made it an important commercial center. Mercantile homeowners who had invested in Baltimore's profitable privateer trade stood to lose a great deal should the British capture and burn the city, which of course, they intended to do.

On the morning of September 12, 1814, before "the first brush of dawn," the British army, with a detachment of seamen and Marines, landed at North Point and began their march towards Baltimore, ten miles away. The British strategy was a joint land and sea offensive. The army, commanded by Major General Robert Ross, was to provide the main attack, while the navy, commanded by Vice-Admiral Cochrane, would bombard Fort McHenry, the keystone of Baltimore's harbor defenses.

To the east of the city at Hampstead Hill, Major General Samuel Smith prepared his mile-long American defense lines held by militia infantry and artillery units of the Third Division, Maryland Volunteer Militia. These lines were to support Commodore John Rodgers, who manned the several artillery redoubts known as "Rodgers' Bastion."

Earlier that morning, Smith sent out the best trained of his militia troop (the 3rd Brigade), commanded by Brigadier General John Stricker, to slow the enemy advance along the North Point Road. The British Army had proceeded only a brief distance when the advance pickets (guards) made initial contact with a company of American riflemen. General Ross, who rode ahead of the main British army with his staff to investigate, was fatally wounded in the skirmish that ensued. "Thus fell," a British officer remembered, "at an early age, one of the brightest ornaments of his profession …" With the death of General Ross, British hopes of capturing Baltimore were severely diminished. The command of the army now rested upon Colonel Arthur Brooke,

OPPOSITE TOP: Major General Samuel Smith (painting by Rembrandt Peale) was the commander of Baltimore's defense. He was also a veteran of the Revolutionary War and a Senator from Maryland. His political influence was important in gaining military funding for the city's defense.
OPPOSITE BOTTOM: *Assembly of Troops on Hampstead Hill,* by Thomas Ruckle, Ca. 1814.

Courtesy of the Maryland Historical Society

an officer "better calculated to lead a battalion, than to guide an army."

The British Light Infantry, passing their fallen commander, was hurried forward, and the Battle of North Point began, lasting a little more than two hours. Volley upon volley of musket and artillery fire between the two lines obscured the field with dense smoke, causing the inexperienced American militia lines on the left to waver under the assault. Fearing a general rout (mass exodus of his troops), General Stricker ordered a withdrawal to the safety of Hampstead Hill, near the city.

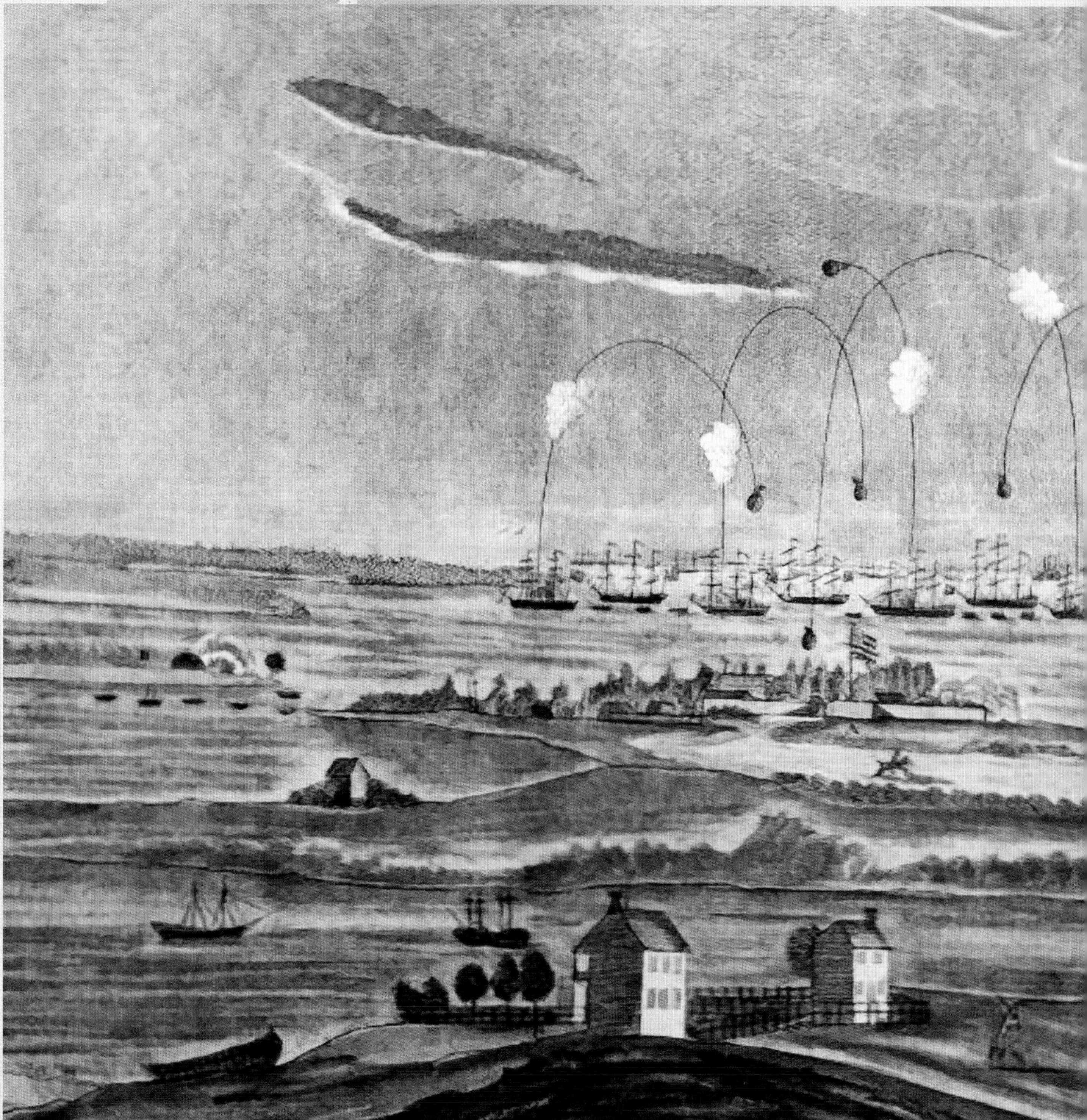

RIGHT: *A View of the Bombardment of Fort McHenry* by John Bower, 1816, (detail).

Approximately 1,000 American soldiers under Major George Armistead's command were ready to defend their new country. Sixteen British ships fired their cannons and guns on Fort McHenry. Congreve rockets from HMS *Erebus* and mortar shells from *Terror, Volcano, Meteor, Devastation* and *Etna* continued to pound the fort. The British naval force withdrew just beyond range of the fort's guns, bombarding Fort McHenry for the next 25 hours. An estimated 1,500 to 1,800 cannonballs did not cause significant damage.

The only light during this bombardment was that from the exploding shells as the city's lights were extinguished during the battle.

During the night, Vice-Admiral Sir Alexander Cochrane ordered small boats to land just west of Fort McHenry in an effort to slip past the fort and draw Major General Samuel Smith's forces away from the eastern defenses. However, they were repulsed by fire from McHenry's guns and other gun batteries along the shore line.

Courtesy of the Maryland Historical Society

ABOVE: *Bombardment of Fort McHenry*, by Alfred Jacob Miller, Ca. 1828-1830.

By evening, as the British army encamped, sixteen British warships began their way up the Patapsco River to take up positions for an attack on Fort McHenry the next morning.

At dawn on September 13, 1814, the British bomb ships *Volcano, Etna, Devastation, Meteor,* and *Terror* began their fiery bombardment of Fort McHenry, exposing the garrison "to a constant and tremendous shower of shells." Each bomb ship was equipped with the most powerful naval weapon of the period— the 13-inch, 8,000-pound sea mortar—capable of hurtling a 194-pound cast-iron bomb shell two and one-half miles. Four or five bombs were frequently in the air at a time. During the 25-hour bombardment, an estimated 1,500 to 2,000 bombs and rockets were fired. The British also employed the 32-pound Congreve Rocket Battery from HMS *Erebus*, but unlike the bombs, they proved ineffective against the Fort. The superior range of the sea mortars enabled the British to keep out of range of the Fort's 36-pounder naval shore batteries.

By noon, heavy rain showers and thunder added to the awesome yet majestic scene the bombardment created. At 2:00 p.m., a British bomb exploded on the southwest bastion of Fort McHenry, dismounting a 24-pound cannon, which killed two men and wounded several others. The confusion caused by this action distracted the men at Fort McHenry, enabling the British to take advantage of the situation by moving their ships closer. The Fort subsequently opened fire, forcing the British to withdraw to their previous position, where they continued the bombardment into the night.

The next morning, as the bombardment began, the British army resumed their march towards Baltimore. An attempt was made that afternoon to flank the American forces left on Hampstead Hill, but this movement was quickly countered. Colonel Brooke then repositioned his army two miles east of the American defenses and awaited naval support, which was deemed necessary in order for the army to launch a successful attack on the American redoubts at 2:00 a.m. the next morning.

The British navy, despite their heavy bombardment of the Fort, and the American blockage of sunken vessels in the harbor entrance to Baltimore, could not bring the ships closer. Near midnight, Admiral Cochrane decided to try another measure to assist the land troops. Approximately twenty British landing barges, equipped with scaling ladders, and smaller support vessels commanded by Captain Charles Napier, moved to the west of Fort McHenry, up the Ferry Branch.

In an effort to entice the Americans to withdraw from Hampstead Hill so that their army could successfully attack the city, the British had a plan to storm and open fire on American shore redoubts behind Fort McHenry at 1:00 a.m. on September 14, 1814. This plan was foiled, however, and the British were driven back by cannon fire from Forts McHenry, Covington, Battery Babcock, and Look-out. On land, Colonel Brooke had serious doubts on success. A council of war soon decided to withdraw the army rather than risk heavy losses without naval support, and began the march back to North Point. The navy continued to bombard Fort McHenry, and covered Captain Napier's retreat until 7:30 a.m. By 9:00 a.m., with the Star-Spangled Banner waving in defiance over Fort McHenry, the British sailed down the Patapsco River. The Battle of Baltimore was over.

The American victory at Baltimore and the timely defeat of the British on Lake Champlain and in Plattsburg, New York on September 10, 1814 enabled the American peace commissioners to conclude the peace talks at Ghent, Belgium and sign the Treaty of Ghent on Christmas Eve, 1814. While the Treaty made its way across the Atlantic to America, Major General Andrew Jackson defeated the British army at New Orleans on January 8th, 1815. On February 17, 1815, the U.S. Congress ratified the Treaty, thus officially ending the War of 1812. Though the Treaty did not settle any of the disputes that had caused the United States and England to fight in the first place, it did bring lasting peace to the two nations.

⭐ NORTH POINT STATE PARK

Near here, at about 3:00 a.m. on September 12, 1814, the British debarked approximately 4,500 troops to attack Baltimore in concert with the naval attack on Fort McHenry. After defeating the Americans at the Battle of North Point, but failing to outflank the city defenses at Hampstead Hill, the troops withdrew and re-embarked here on September 15, 1814. The Park is also home to Todd's Inheritance where an American signal/horse courier was stationed to report British movements to Baltimore. In retaliation for these activities, the British burned the house during the Battle of North Point on September 12, 1814; the present 1816 house replaces the original.

A Chesapeake Bay Gateways Network Site
www.dnrstate.md.us/publiclands/central/northpoint.html

⭐ BATTLE ACRE

This acre was dedicated on the 25th anniversary of the Battle of North Point in 1839 with a ceremony that culminated with the spreading out of the Star-Spangled Banner. The monument, completed in 1914, is near where the 5th Maryland Regiment was positioned during the Battle of North Point, September 12, 1814.
www.battlenorthpoint.org

⭐ FORT McHENRY NATIONAL MONUMENT AND HISTORIC SHRINE

Fort McHenry served as the cornerstone of the water defenses of Baltimore during the Battle of Baltimore on September 12-14, 1814. It was over this fort that the Star-Spangled Banner flew, inspiring Francis Scott Key to write the poem that became our National Anthem.
A Chesapeake Bay Gateways Network Site
www.nps.gov/fomc

⭐ STAR-SPANGLED BANNER FLAG HOUSE

Here, Mary Young Pickersgill, at the request of Major George Armistead, sewed Fort McHenry's large garrison flag and the smaller storm flag, which flew over the fort during the famous bombardment. The Museum displays artifacts from the Battle of North Point and plays host to several living history events.
www.flaghouse.org

⭐ FELL'S POINT

The British referred to Baltimore as a "nest of pirates," and it was partly to punish Baltimore for its privateering industry, centered in Fell's Point, that the British mounted their attack on Baltimore in September 1814.
A Chesapeake Bay Gateways Network Site

⭐ *PRIDE OF BALTIMORE II*

This reproduction of a Baltimore Clipper represents the sleek, daring 'privateers' that were the life blood of the fledgling American nation during the War of 1812. Ships like the *Pride II* fought against the largest armada of fighting ships ever assembled. Today, the *Pride II* is berthed at Baltimore's Inner Harbor when she is not sailing the world as Maryland's Goodwill Ambassador.
A Chesapeake Bay Gateways Network Site
www.marylandspride.org

ABOVE: *Fifth Maryland Regiment, Battle of North Point, September 12, 1814* by Don Troiani, 1982

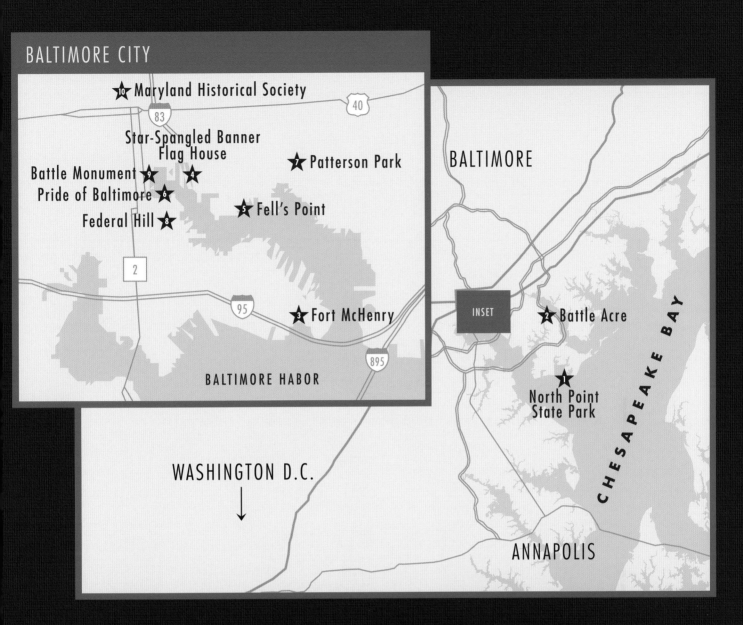

Maryland Historical Society

Star-Spangled Banner Flag House

Patterson Park

Battle Monument

Pride of Baltimore

Fell's Point

Federal Hill

Fort McHenry

BALTIMORE HABOR

WASHINGTON D.C.

BALTIMORE

INSET

Battle Acre

North Point State Park

CHESAPEAKE BAY

ANNAPOLIS

☆ PATTERSON PARK

It was here at Hampstead Hill, on September 13, 1814, that the British were stopped in their tracks as they approached Baltimore. When British Col. Brooke realized that the Royal Navy could not help take Hampstead Hill, he and his forces marched back to North Point where they re-embarked their ships.
www.pattersonpark.com

☆ FEDERAL HILL

On this hill, overlooking the Inner Harbor, a one-gun battery fired in quick succession three shots signaling the British had landed at North Point. It was also from here many citizens watched the bombardment of Fort McHenry, September 13-14, 1814.
www.historicfederalhill.org

☆ BATTLE MONUMENT

This 52-foot-tall monument, the first substantial war memorial built in the United States, was erected to commemorate the citizens of the city who fell during the Battle of Baltimore. The cornerstone was laid on September 12, 1815, the first anniversary of the Battle of North Point, and completed in 1829, when it became the official seal of the City of Baltimore.
www.nps.gov/history/hdp/exhibits/baltimore/B2L02.pdf

☆ MARYLAND HISTORICAL SOCIETY

Among its many exhibits are paintings, prints and artifacts from the Battle of Baltimore, including the earliest original manuscript version of Francis Scott Key's poem, which ultimately became the words to the National Anthem.
www.mdhs.org

Biography

FRANCIS SCOTT KEY

Francis Scott Key was born in 1779 in Frederick County, shortly before the end of the War for Independence. He is representative of the first generation of Americans who never experienced life as a colonist. The early years of his life corresponded with the formative years of the United States. He graduated from Saint John's College in Annapolis in 1796 and began his legal career as an apprentice to his uncle, Philip Barton Key.

In 1805 he moved his family to Georgetown. Key's legal career grew over time. In 1807 he defended two associates of Aaron Burr who were accused of treason. Tried before the U.S. Supreme Court, they were found not guilty. While his law practice foundered during the War of 1812 his practice recovered and he was appointed District Attorney for Washington, D.C. by President Andrew Jackson in 1833. As a prosecutor in the case U.S. v. Reuben Crandall in 1836, he defended the rights of slaveholders and described abolitionists as "men of most horrid principles, whose means of attack upon us are insurrection, tumult and violence." Like many affluent Southerners, Key was a slaveholder, however he freed some of his enslaved workforce. He acknowledged the evil of slavery but believed its sudden abolition would result in social chaos.

In addition to being the author of "The Star-Spangled Banner" and a successful lawyer, Key was the father of six boys and five girls. His wife, Mary Tayloe Lloyd, was 18 years old when they married. Key took particular interest in the education of his children. He entertained them by writing poems and stories. His letters to them stress education and religious faith. A devout Episcopalian, Key served as a trustee for the General Theological Seminary, the oldest seminary of the Episcopal Church, from its founding in 1820 until 1843. He wrote a number of religious songs, some of which are still sung today.

O say can you see ~~through~~ by the dawn's early light,
What so proudly we hail'd at the twilight's last gleaming,
Whose broad stripes & bright stars through the perilous fight
O'er the ramparts we watch'd, were so gallantly streaming?
And the rocket's red glare, the bomb bursting in air,
Gave proof through the night that our flag was still there,
O say does that star spangled banner yet wave
O'er the land of the free & the home of the brave?

On the shore dimly seen through the mists of the deep,
Where the foe's haughty host in dread silence reposes,
What is that which the breeze, o'er the towering steep,
As it fitfully blows, half conceals, half discloses?
Now it catches the gleam of the morning's first beam,
In full glory reflected now shines in the stream,
'Tis the star-spangled banner — O long may it wave
O'er the land of the free & the home of the brave!

And where is that band who so vauntingly swore,
That the havoc of war & the battle's confusion
A home & a Country should leave us no more?
~~Their blood~~
Their blood has wash'd out their foul footstep's pollution.
No refuge could save the hireling & slave
From the terror of flight or the gloom of the grave,
And the star-spangled banner in triumph doth wave
O'er the land of the free & the home of the brave.

O thus be it ever when freemen shall stand
Between their lov'd home & the war's desolation!
Blest with vict'ry & peace may the heav'n rescued land
Praise the power that hath made & preserv'd us a nation!
Then conquer we must, when our cause it is just,
And this be our motto — "In God is our trust,"
And the star-spangled banner in triumph shall wave
O'er the land of the free & the home of the brave. —

Lyrics

THE STAR-SPANGLED BANNER

O, say can you see by the dawn's early light
What so proudly we hailed at the twilight's last gleaming?
Whose broad stripes and bright stars thru the perilous fight,
O'er the ramparts we watched were so gallantly streaming?
And the rocket's red glare, the bombs bursting in air,
Gave proof through the night that our flag was still there.
Oh, say does that star-spangled banner yet wave
O'er the land of the free and the home of the brave?

On the shore, dimly seen through the mists of the deep,
Where the foe's haughty host in dread silence reposes,
What is that which the breeze, o'er the towering steep,
As it fitfully blows, half conceals, half discloses?
Now it catches the gleam of the morning's first beam,
In full glory reflected now shines in the stream:
'Tis the star-spangled banner! Oh long may it wave
O'er the land of the free and the home of the brave!

And where is that band who so vauntingly swore
That the havoc of war and the battle's confusion,
A home and a country should leave us no more!
Their blood has washed out their foul footsteps' pollution.
No refuge could save the hireling and slave
From the terror of flight, or the gloom of the grave:
And the star-spangled banner in triumph doth wave
O'er the land of the free and the home of the brave!

Oh! thus be it ever, when freemen shall stand
Between their loved home and the war's desolation!
Blest with victory and peace, may the heav'n rescued land
Praise the Power that hath made and preserved us a nation.
Then conquer we must, when our cause it is just,
And this be our motto: "In God is our trust."
And the star-spangled banner in triumph shall wave
O'er the land of the free and the home of the brave!

LEFT: The complete poem and lyrics of "The Star-Spangled Banner"

OPPOSITE: Francis Scott Key watches the bombardment of Fort McHenry from aboard an American truce ship in the harbor. *By Dawn's Early Light,* Edward Percy Moran, oil on canvas, 1912.

THE STAR-SPANGLED BANNER FLAG

In the summer of 1813, Major George Armistead made an unusual inquiry to General Samuel Smith: "We, Sir, are ready at Fort McHenry to defend Baltimore … except that we have no suitable ensign to display over the Star Fort, and it is my desire to have a flag so large that the British will have no difficulty in seeing it from a distance."

Armistead's request was taken to No. 60 Albemarle Street, the home of Mary Young Pickersgill, a maker of flags in Baltimore. The flag,

BELOW: Star-Spangled Banner Flag House

Photo © Coolcaesar/Wikipedia

which was made of woolen bunting, measured 30 feet by 42 feet and had 15 stars and stripes. The stripes were two feet wide and the stars were two feet from point to point. Mary and her 13-year-old daughter, Caroline, worked in an upstairs front bedroom, using 400 yards of the best quality fabric. They laid out the fabric on the malthouse floor of Claggett's Brewery and sewed it there. In addition, a smaller storm flag was made, which measured 17 feet by 25 feet. On August 19, 1813, a full year before the Battle of Baltimore, both flags were delivered to Fort McHenry at a cost of $574.44.

A year later, in 1814 as the British army left a burning Washington behind, Dr. William Beanes, an American civilian and much-loved town physician, was taken captive at his home in Upper Marlboro, Maryland for having arrested and imprisoned some British soldiers, one of whom escaped. The British, who had earlier established their temporary headquarters in Beanes' home prior to Bladensburg and had received the doctor's pledge of neutrality, now considered his actions a breach of faith. The elderly doctor was taken from his home and sequestered aboard the British warship *Tonnant*.

Key quickly made preparations to obtain the release of his friend, and after obtaining the proper letters of introduction proceeded to Baltimore where he enlisted the services of Colonel John Skinner, the government's official prisoner of war exchanges agent. On September 5, they departed Baltimore on a small packet-sloop flying a flag of truce. Two days later they met the British fleet in the Chesapeake Bay.

At first, the British refused to release Dr. Beanes. Key and Skinner produced several letters written by British prisoners praising the treatment they were receiving by doctors, among them, Dr. Beanes. Arrangements for Dr. Beanes' release were quickly obtained, but due to the impeding attack on Baltimore, the men were detained for security reasons. On September 10th, as the British fleet reached the Patapsco River near North Point, they were sent back aboard the American vessel, under British guard. Key, Skinner, and Dr. Beanes watched the fiery bombardment of Fort McHenry from the main British anchorage eight miles away, which started at 7:00 a.m., September 13th. The bombardment continued for 25 hours with the British firing 1,500 bombshells. Close approach was not possible as Baltimore merchants had purposely sunk a number of their vessels to block the channel.

The three men knew that as long as the shelling continued, Fort McHenry had not surrendered. But the British lit up the night sky with their exploding bombs and the red glare of their rockets. When the bombing subsided, what they didn't know was who had won. Key anxiously waited in the darkness for the answer.

This question of whether or not Baltimore had fallen was answered when daylight came the morning of September 14th. Over the earthen and brick ramparts of Fort McHenry, Major Armistead's flag of defiance could be seen as the Fort's morning gun was fired and the fifes and drums played "Yankee Doodle."

Moved by the sight of the flag still flying above Fort McHenry, Key, an amateur poet, was inspired to write a few poetic verses. He began writing on the back of a letter in his pocket. Upon his release and return to Baltimore on September 16th, Key completed his poem at the Indian Queen Tavern. The following day, it was printed on a handbill under the title, "Defence of Fort McHenry." Two of these copies survive today. On September 20th, it was published in a Baltimore newspaper. The title was soon changed to "The Star-Spangled Banner."

The popularity of Francis Scott Key's new national song, which was being sung to the tune of "To Anacreon in Heaven," grew over the years as the nation prospered in war and peace. Through the patriotic efforts of concerned Marylanders, Congress made "The Star-Spangled Banner" the official national anthem on March 3, 1931. It is one of the few national anthems in the world devoted to a flag.

BELOW: Shreds of the Star-Spangled Banner on exhibit at the Smithsonian Institution's National Museum of American History

OPPOSITE PAGE: The original Star-Spangled Banner

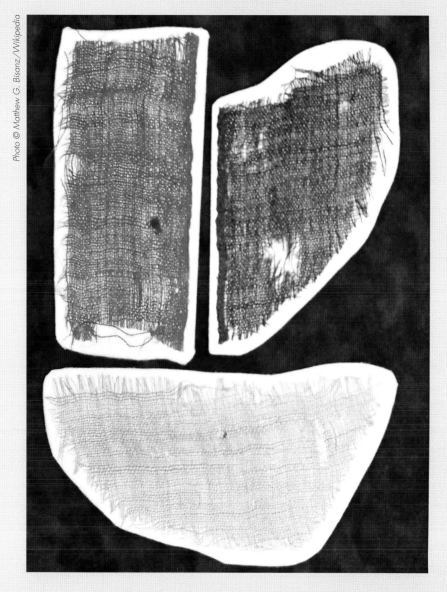

THE STAR-SPANGLED BANNER FLAG TODAY

The original flag is among the most treasured pieces of history today. It is housed in the Smithsonian's National Museum of American History in Washington, D.C.

When Armistead's widow died in 1861, the Star-Spangled Banner was inherited by his daughter, Georgiana Armistead Appleton. Georgiana recognized that it held great national significance and she allowed the flag be exhibited on many occasions. Her son, Eben Appleton inherited the flag upon his mother's death in 1878. As the public became more interested in the Star-Spangled Banner, Eben decided to find an appropriate home for it. In 1912, he gifted the flag to the nation. He wrote, "It is always such a satisfaction to me to feel that the flag is just where it is, in possession for all time of the very best custodian, where it is beautifully displayed and can be conveniently seen by so many people."

The Armistead family had received many requests for pieces of the flag. Over 200 square feet, including one star, has been given away, mostly to veterans, honored citizens and government officials. In 1914, the flag was displayed in a glass case in the Smithsonian's Arts and Industries Building for almost 50 years. The exception was during World War II. It was housed for two years in a government warehouse in Virginia to protect it from potential bombing on the nation's capital. A new home was given to the flag in 1964 in the new National Museum of History and Technology in the central hall on the second floor. This is now the National Museum of American History.

A plan to conserve the flag was under way in 1994. The Star-Spangled Banner's most recent preservation effort was its inclusion in "Save America's Treasures," a Millennium preservation project. In 1999, the flag was taken down from the wall for the first time since 1964. After a lengthy period of conservation work was completed, the restored flag was placed in a new climate- and light-controlled exhibit area where it can be seen today.

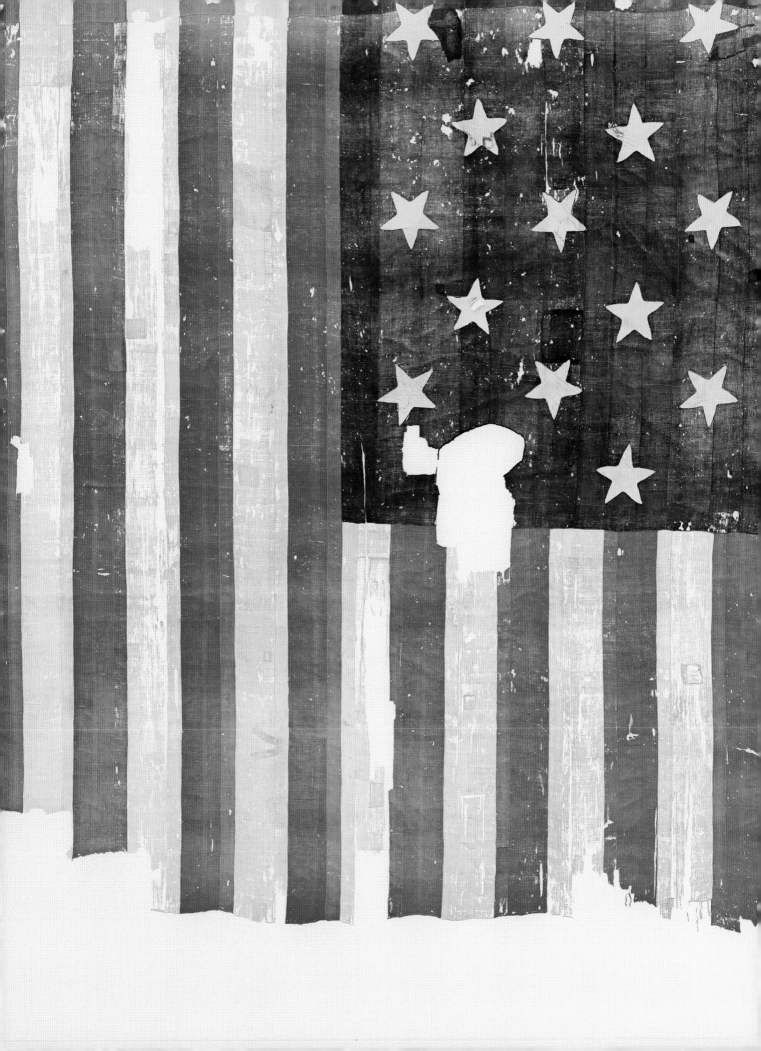

History
OF THE AMERICAN FLAG

The design of the Stars and Stripes as a national flag came from a committee formed by Congress in 1776. Although no single individual is credited with designing the entire flag, research indicates that Congressman Francis Hopkinson designed most of it. Many historians do not believe that Betsy Ross, invented the flag or made the first one, although it has been proven that she did exist, lived in Philadelphia and was by profession, a flag-maker. As the country grew, the flag has changed 26 times since the 13-star banner was authorized on June 14, 1777.

As American nationalism grew in the 1800s and early 1900s, so did the flag as a symbol of our nation's pride and unity. It is widely recognized as a representation of our government and of the nation's ideals. Its association with "The Star-Spangled Banner" made it even more popular. During the Civil War and all succeeding military conflicts, the Stars and Stripes was a rallying point for both the armed forces and civilians.

In 1942, an earlier Flag Code, establishing guidance for handling and proper display of the flag, became a federal law. By the 1960s the American flag was seen by some to reflect a narrow and exclusive vision of American identity. In protest they burned and defaced flags, prompting Congress to criminalize such behavior in 1968. This legislation was repealed after the Supreme Court ruled in 1989 that flag burning was an expression of freedom of speech. These struggles over the flag's meaning are testaments to its enduring power as a national symbol and icon.

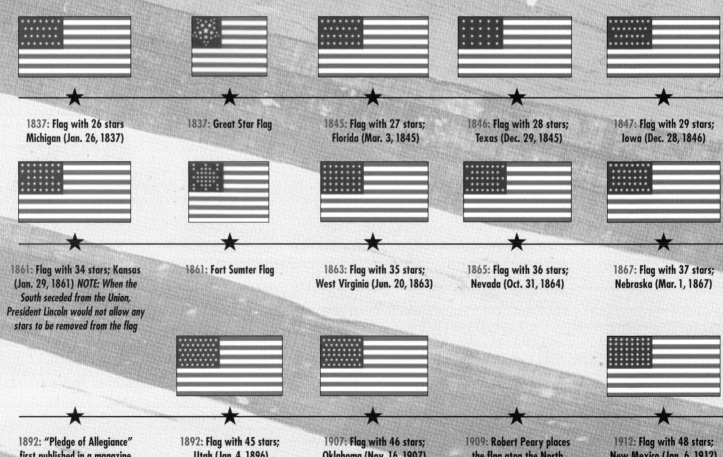

1837: Flag with 26 stars Michigan (Jan. 26, 1837)

1837: Great Star Flag

1845: Flag with 27 stars; Florida (Mar. 3, 1845)

1846: Flag with 28 stars; Texas (Dec. 29, 1845)

1847: Flag with 29 stars; Iowa (Dec. 28, 1846)

1861: Flag with 34 stars; Kansas (Jan. 29, 1861) *NOTE: When the South seceded from the Union, President Lincoln would not allow any stars to be removed from the flag*

1861: Fort Sumter Flag

1863: Flag with 35 stars; West Virginia (Jun. 20, 1863)

1865: Flag with 36 stars; Nevada (Oct. 31, 1864)

1867: Flag with 37 stars; Nebraska (Mar. 1, 1867)

1892: "Pledge of Allegiance" first published in a magazine called "The Youth's Companion," written by Francis Bellamy.

1892: Flag with 45 stars; Utah (Jan. 4, 1896)

1907: Flag with 46 stars; Oklahoma (Nov. 16, 1907)

1909: Robert Peary places the flag atop the North Pole. He left fragments of it as he traveled north.

1912: Flag with 48 stars; New Mexico (Jan. 6, 1912), Arizona (Feb. 14, 1912)

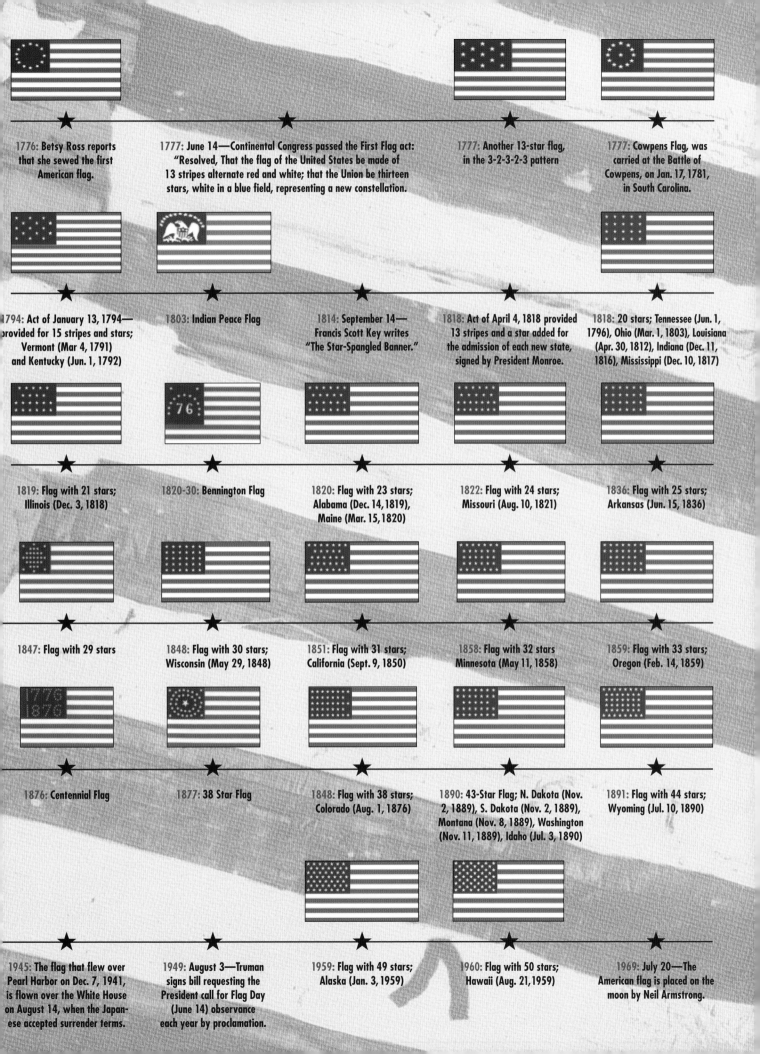

1776: Betsy Ross reports that she sewed the first American flag.

1777: June 14—Continental Congress passed the First Flag act: "Resolved, That the flag of the United States be made of 13 stripes alternate red and white; that the Union be thirteen stars, white in a blue field, representing a new constellation."

1777: Another 13-star flag, in the 3-2-3-2-3 pattern

1777: Cowpens Flag, was carried at the Battle of Cowpens, on Jan. 17, 1781, in South Carolina.

1794: Act of January 13, 1794—provided for 15 stripes and stars; Vermont (Mar 4, 1791) and Kentucky (Jun. 1, 1792)

1803: Indian Peace Flag

1814: September 14—Francis Scott Key writes "The Star-Spangled Banner."

1818: Act of April 4, 1818 provided 13 stripes and a star added for the admission of each new state, signed by President Monroe.

1818: 20 stars; Tennessee (Jun. 1, 1796), Ohio (Mar. 1, 1803), Louisiana (Apr. 30, 1812), Indiana (Dec. 11, 1816), Mississippi (Dec. 10, 1817)

1819: Flag with 21 stars; Illinois (Dec. 3, 1818)

1820-30: Bennington Flag

1820: Flag with 23 stars; Alabama (Dec. 14, 1819), Maine (Mar. 15, 1820)

1822: Flag with 24 stars; Missouri (Aug. 10, 1821)

1836: Flag with 25 stars; Arkansas (Jun. 15, 1836)

1847: Flag with 29 stars

1848: Flag with 30 stars; Wisconsin (May 29, 1848)

1851: Flag with 31 stars; California (Sept. 9, 1850)

1858: Flag with 32 stars Minnesota (May 11, 1858)

1859: Flag with 33 stars; Oregon (Feb. 14, 1859)

1876: Centennial Flag

1877: 38 Star Flag

1848: Flag with 38 stars; Colorado (Aug. 1, 1876)

1890: 43-Star Flag; N. Dakota (Nov. 2, 1889), S. Dakota (Nov. 2, 1889), Montana (Nov. 8, 1889), Washington (Nov. 11, 1889), Idaho (Jul. 3, 1890)

1891: Flag with 44 stars; Wyoming (Jul. 10, 1890)

1945: The flag that flew over Pearl Harbor on Dec. 7, 1941, is flown over the White House on August 14, when the Japanese accepted surrender terms.

1949: August 3—Truman signs bill requesting the President call for Flag Day (June 14) observance each year by proclamation.

1959: Flag with 49 stars; Alaska (Jan. 3, 1959)

1960: Flag with 50 stars; Hawaii (Aug. 21,1959)

1969: July 20—The American flag is placed on the moon by Neil Armstrong.

Part 3
POST-WAR ACTIVITY, 1815-PRESENT

Following the War of 1812, Fort McHenry, like other coastal fortifications, underwent gradual development as new, powerful weapons and military strategies rendered these earlier defenses obsolete. As Baltimore and other nearby cities grew and commercial growth increased, additional protection was deemed necessary. Thus, no sooner had the bombardment of Fort McHenry ended, than the Fort's powder magazine was enlarged to "its present dimensions, and two personnel bomb-proofs (a thick-walled structure that can withstand the penetration of bombs) were built—one on each side of the Fort's sally port (entranceway).

In 1829, modifications were made to Fort McHenry's 1814-period structures that we view today. Newer and stronger gun batteries were built that served Fort McHenry during the Civil War years. During the Mexican War (1846-1848) the Fort's expanded grounds, purchased in 1836, were utilized as a recruiting and training center for Maryland troops before they were sent south of the border.

Although Fort McHenry's strategic importance earlier in the century was declining, a small "caretaker" garrison (the group of soldiers stationed to a fort) remained.

By 1860, slavery, state's rights, and the complex political issues confronting an expanding country threatened to divide the country in a war between the states.

BELOW: The mammoth Rodman cannons represent one of the most complete collections of Civil War-era seacoast cannons in the United States. **OPPOSITE PAGE:** A replica of the 15-star and 15-stripe flag flies over Fort McHenry. By a Presidential Proclamation issued by President Truman in 1948, a flag of the United States flies over the birthplace of the American national anthem 24 hours a day. It is spotlighted at night by solar powered lighting.

Photo by Joe Luman © Terrell Creative

THE CIVIL WAR YEARS, 1861-1865

During the Civil War, Fort McHenry played a key role in providing the federal government with a military base of operations to suppress civil rebellion and subsequently, as the various campaigns centered around Maryland, a convenient detention site for political prisoners as well as thousands of captured Confederate soldiers.

On April 19, 1861, the first civil clash of arms occurred when Baltimoreans protested the passage of northern troops through the city. These troops were responding to President Lincoln's call for 75,000 volunteers following the bombardment of Fort Sumter in South Carolina. The protest was known as the Pratt Street Riot,

and it symbolized the divided views within the state. Shortly thereafter the fort's cannons were aimed at Baltimore City.

It soon became evident that Baltimore's central location was important in securing vital communication lines to Washington. By the summer of 1861, thousands of Union troops had occupied and fortified Baltimore. During the Gettysburg campaign in 1863, nearly 7,000 Confederate soldiers were imprisoned at Fort McHenry before being transferred to other more permanent prisons. The grandsons of Francis Scott Key and Major Armistead, as well as members of the city and state governments were among those civilians imprisoned at the Fort for their suspected southern sympathies.

The occupation of Fort McHenry during the Civil War was remembered by many

Marylanders as the "Baltimore Bastille," an ironic twist of history considering what had occurred there during the War of 1812 a half century before.

A FINAL FAREWELL

Following the Civil War, more improvements were made that reflect the Fort's present-day appearance. Rodman cannons, made standard seacoast ordinance in 1861, were finally mounted in the Fort's outer battery. The Rodman gun represented state-of-the-art technology in the era of muzzle-loading, smoothbore artillery, which had governed warfare for hundreds of years. By the turn of the 19th century, these guns became obsolete.

On July 20, 1912, the 141st Company of Coastal Artillery, the last active garrison, departed, leaving only memories of Fort McHenry's nearly 125 years of active service to the country. Two years later Marylanders held centennial observances of the Battle of Baltimore and erected a statue to the Fort's commander, Major George Armistead.

In 1917, the U.S. Army returned in unprecedented numbers as U.S. General Hospital No. 2 was erected on the grounds surrounding the old Fort. Over 100 buildings and nearly 3,000 hospital beds were built to serve the wounded soldiers returning from the battlefields of Europe during World War I. Medical history in the fields of neurosurgery and plastic surgery was made at Fort McHenry, enabling many soldiers to return home. By 1925, the last patients had left, the hospital was torn down, and Fort McHenry became a national park under the administration of the U.S. Army. During the 1920s, the U.S. Army restored the Fort to its pre-Civil War appearance.

"The Star-Spangled Banner" became one of the country's most beloved patriotic songs. During the Civil War, it was especially popular as many Americans wanted to express their emotions for the ideals and values it represented. The military began using the song for ceremonial purposes by the 1890s. It was required to be played at the raising and lowering of the flag. The army and the navy designated it as the national anthem for their ceremonies. Patriotic organizations had launched a campaign for Congress to recognize "The Star-Spangled Banner" as the U.S. national anthem. After many decades of attempts, it was officially adopted as our national anthem on March 31, 1931 and in 1933 the U.S. Army transferred Fort McHenry and its 43 additional acres to the management of the National Park Service. The park's designation changed from national park to national monument and historic shrine in 1939.

BELOW: Nurses and medical staff attend a ceremony in the Star Fort during World War 1.
OPPOSITE: *Baltimore Riot of 1861* Engraving by R.R. Walker (1861)

Courtesy National Park Service

During World War II, the secretary of the navy assigned the U.S. Coast Guard to protect the nation's port facilities. From 1942-1945, the Fort McHenry Coast Guard Fire Training Station was responsible for making security patrols and for teaching ship-board fire techniques.

Today, nearly one million visitors from all parts of the world visit the park annually. A wide variety of activities are provided by park rangers during the summer months. From Memorial Day through Labor Day, the Fort's long, active military history is presented in various interpretive activities. Flag Day is celebrated on June 14th, and in September the annual Star-Spangled Banner Weekend celebration marks the traditional anniversary of the Battle of Baltimore and the writing of "The Star-Spangled Banner." Dressed in period costume, the Fort McHenry Guard provides a glimpse into the summer of 1814 with military demonstrations, drills and special ceremonies.

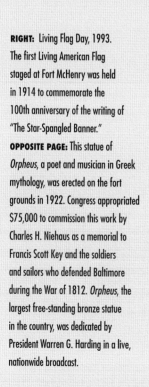

RIGHT: Living Flag Day, 1993. The first Living American Flag staged at Fort McHenry was held in 1914 to commemorate the 100th anniversary of the writing of "The Star-Spangled Banner."

OPPOSITE PAGE: This statue of *Orpheus*, a poet and musician in Greek mythology, was erected on the fort grounds in 1922. Congress appropriated $75,000 to commission this work by Charles H. Niehaus as a memorial to Francis Scott Key and the soldiers and sailors who defended Baltimore during the War of 1812. *Orpheus*, the largest free-standing bronze statue in the country, was dedicated by President Warren G. Harding in a live, nationwide broadcast.

ABOVE: The curved walls in Fort McHenry's Visitor and Education Center evoke the furling of the flag. The walls, one of zinc and one of brick, represent the white and red stripes of the flag.

A chance to experience the bombs bursting in air awaits visitors in the 17,655-square-foot Fort McHenry Visitor and Education Center. The highly interactive experience takes visitors as closely back to the War of 1812 and the Battle of Baltimore as possible. The museum-quality interpretative center features graphics, interactive exhibits and artifacts.

Francis Scott Key is the subject of the largest gallery. Here visitors can examine his handwriting, noting the early drafts of his poem and how he changed certain words. A film about the War of 1812 and Baltimore's role is presented on a giant screen. A curtain slowly rises at the end revealing to the audience the panoramic view of the fort. In the center stands a replica of Armistead's flag proudly flying, a scene perhaps similar to what Key saw that fateful morning at dawn.

Photo by Kelly Elliott © Terrell Creative

Photo by Kelly Elliott © Terrell Creative

ABOVE AND LEFT: In the first level of the center is a museum-quality interpretive center with interactive exhibits, graphics, artifacts and a film. At the end of the film, the screen disappears to reveal the outside view of the fort and the flag.

LEFT: A life-sized bronze statue of Francis Scott Key

Photo by Kelly Elliott © Terrell Creative

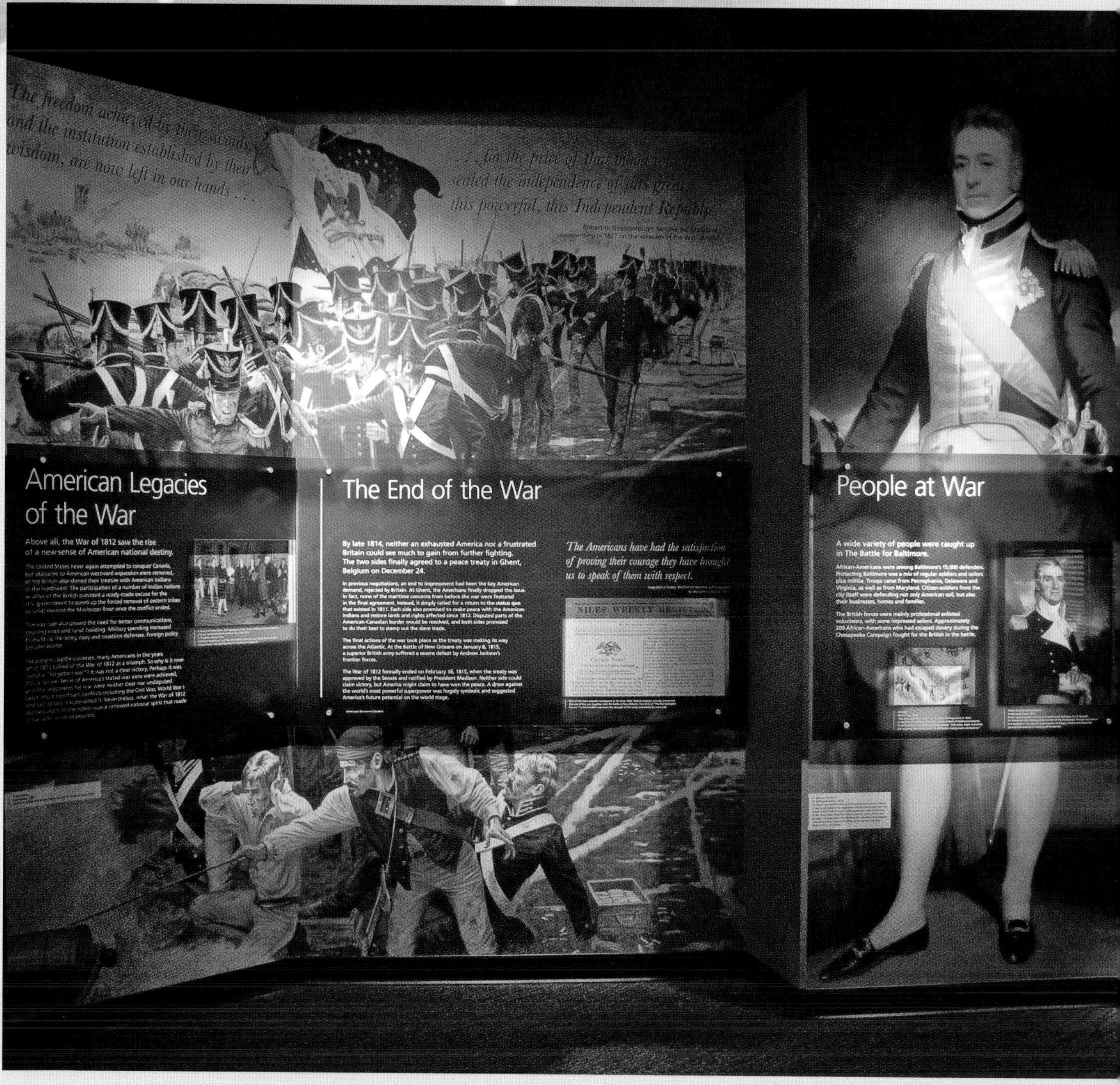

LEFT: Cannons fired cannon balls from six pounds to 36 pounds.

OPPOSITE PAGE AND BELOW: The interpretive center's exhibit space is divided into three galleries that explore the causes of the War of 1812, Francis Scott Key's experience and how the anthem and the flag together became the meaningful symbols they are today.

Patriotism and Place

Fort McHenry provides a unique touchstone both to the dramatic origins of the National Anthem and to American identity.

A Song for America

The words of "The Star-Spangled Banner" are lovely; they are an inspiration from start to finish . . . God bless Francis Scott Key.

The war has raised our reputation in Europe . . . and it excites astonishment that we should have been able for one campaign to have fought Great Britain single handed. . . . I think it will be a long time before we are disturbed again by any of the powers of Europe.

James Bayard, American negotiator, in a letter to his son, December 22, 1814

Triumphs and Catastrophes

Visitors can hear 10 different interpretations of the national anthem, from the Duke Ellington Orchestra's to the version played by Jimi Hendrix at Woodstock.

Fort McHenry is the only National Park Service site that is designated both a national monument and a historic shrine. It is tradition when a new flag is designed for use in the United States, it is first flown over Fort McHenry. Here, the nation demonstrated that Americans united not only to win independence, but to fight to keep it.

ABOVE: Exhibits interpret the complex events that led to the war, the war itself and its results.
RIGHT: Scale model of the Baltimore schooner *Chasseur*. Also known as "The Pride of Baltimore," this ship captured or sank 18 British ships.